Introduction

This book is written in an outline format. It provides clear, concise and detailed information related to job searches and meeting expectations in the workplace. It also shares tips for managing your finances and monitoring your credit.

Table of Contents

Resumes

Do I Need A Resume?
- ☐ If you are looking for a job - you will need a resume

- ☐ What is a resume?
    - ■ A resume is a career marketing tool
        - ☐ A resume communicates your education, skills and experience (work and volunteer) to potential employers
    - ■ A resume can help you to obtain job interviews

- ☐ What personal information should be included on my resume?
    - ■ First and last name
    - ■ Address
    - ■ Telephone number
        - ☐ Cell or home telephone number
            - ☐ You should have a professional voicemail greeting (first and last name)
                - ☐ Avoid using slang phrases
            - ☐ Avoid waiting music

- ☐ Email Address
    - ■ Create an email account for your job search (you can use a free email account Gmail & yahoo)

- ☐ What should I include about my education?
    - ■ Include the name of your current school
    - ■ The state
    - ■ Your expected date of graduation
    - ■ Your major
        - ☐ Business, Computer Science, Technology
    - ■ GPA (is optional)
    - ■ Achievements
        - ☐ Honor roll
        - ☐ Awards and certificates
        - ☐ Clubs and school activities
            - ☐ Basketball team, yearbook, chess club

- ☐ What should I include about my work and volunteer experience?

- ☐ The names of the companies/organizations
    - ■ List paid work separately from volunteer work
    - ■ List your experiences in date order
        - ☐ Most recent on top

- ☐ The dates of your work
    - ■ September 2011 – April 2012

- ☐ Your position
    - ■ Intern
    - ■ Sales clerk
    - ■ Volunteer office worker

- ☐ A description of your assignments
    - ■ Use bullet points and brief descriptions

- ☐ What should I include about my activities and skills?
    - ■ You should include activities that you have participated
    - ■ Charity events and fundraisers

- ☐ Skills
    - ■ Computer programs such as Microsoft Word, Excel, PowerPoint, Photoshop
    - ■ Languages that you can read, write and speak

Resume Layout

- ☐ Grammar
    - ☐ Spell check your resume
    - ☐ Use the correct verb tenses
        - ■ Present tense for current jobs
        - ■ Past tense for former jobs

- ☐ Formatting Consistency
    - ☐ Select one format for displaying dates
        - ■ 9/10 – 6/11 or September 2010 – June 2011
        - ■ If you bold one of the names of an employer, you must bold the names of all employers
        - ■ Use the same font and font size

Important Things to Remember About Your Resume

- [ ] Resume length
    - No longer than 1 page

- [ ] Resume paper
    - Be conservative with your color choice
        - [ ] Use white, off white, ivory

- [ ] Proofread your resume
    - Check spell the entire resume
    - Confirm dates are accurate
    - Confirm the spelling of companies

- [ ] Ask a teacher, parent/guardian or mentor to review your resume before sending it to potential employers

- [ ] Select references before sending out your resume
    - [ ] Obtain approval to use people as a reference

Social Media
- [ ] Social Media – make sure your Facebook page and other social media pages are private

- ❑ Be selective about your social media friends and the information published on under your name

- ❑ Remove inappropriate pictures

- ❑ Remove inappropriate comments/posts

Interview Preparation

What Is An Interview?

- [ ] An interview is a meeting between an employer and a prospective employee
  - During this meeting the employer (the interviewer) will ask the job seeker (the interviewee) a series of questions about
    - [ ] Work/volunteer experience
    - [ ] Education
    - [ ] Skills
    - [ ] Activities and interests
  - These questions are asked to determine if the job seeker will be suitable for the position

- [ ] The interview also presents the job seeker with the opportunity to determine if they are interested in working for the employer

How to Prepare For an Interview

- [ ] Research the company
  - You should be prepared to discuss what you know about the company during your interview
    - [ ] Visit the company's website
    - [ ] Read internet articles

- ☐ Know your resume
    - ■ Be prepared to answer questions about the information on your resume

- ☐ Limit access to your social media pages
    - ■ Make your pages private
    - ■ Do not friend or give access to people you do not know

- ☐ Plan your travel
    - ■ Make sure you know where the company is located
    - ■ Plan how you will travel to the company in advance
        - ☐ Bus, train or walk
        - ☐ Know how long it will take you to travel

- ☐ Have extra copies of your resume
    - ■ You may interview with more than one person
        - ☐ This will show that you are prepared and serious about the position

- ☐ Prepare your clothes before the interview
    - ■ Make sure your interview clothing is clean, ironed and ready to wear the night before your interview

- ■ Make sure your shoes and other accessories are prepared the night before your interview

- ☐ On the day of your interview
    - ■ Turn off your cell phone before you meet your interviewer

Interview Attire

- ☐ Select solid colors for your attire
    - ☐ Navy blue, black, grey or dark brown
    - ■ Wear a suit
        - ☐ If you do not have a suit
            - ☐ Wear a dress pants
            - ☐ Wear a conservative skirt
    - ■ Shirts or blouses
        - ☐ White is the most conservative color
    - ■ Belt
        - ☐ Should be navy blue, black, grey or dark brown
- ☐ Interview Attire
    - ■ Tie
        - ☐ Should be conservative colors
        - ☐ Solid colors and no designs (to be conservative)
    - ■ Shoes

- ☐ Conservative colors
    - ☐ Ladies – flats or low heels
    - ☐ Men loafers or tie shoes
  - ☐ No boots, athletic foot wear or sandals

- ☐ Make sure you are well rested before your interview
  - ■ Get a goodnight sleep
    - ☐ This will help you to appear alert during your interview

- ☐ Arrive early for your interview
  - ■ Be prepared for unexpected travel delays
    - ☐ Leave the house earlier

- ☐ If you are going to be late, please call your interviewer
  - ■ Do not leave the house without your interviewer's contact information
  - ■ Telephone number and address

- ☐ Shake the interview's hand when introduced
  - ■ Use your right hand
  - ■ Your hand shake should be firm, but not forceful

- ☐ Do not wave hi

- ☐ Your body language will speak for itself
  - ◼ It will tell an interview whether you are interested in the position
  - ◼ Focused on the conversation
    - ☐ Be sure to make eye contact with your interviewer
  - ◼ Sit up straight in your chair
  - ◼ Do not fidget or bite your nails
  - ◼ Look at your interviewer
  - ◼ Do not look around the room
  - ◼ Do not look down at the table

- ☐ Speak clearly and loud enough for the interviewer to hear you
  - ◼ Do not mumble
  - ◼ Do not whisper
  - ◼ Do not shake your head (yes or no) in response to questions
- ☐ Ask questions
  - ◼ About the position
  - ◼ The duties associated with the position
  - ◼ The company

- ☐ End the interview with a positive statement
  - ◼ I look forward to hearing from you
  - ◼ Thank the interviewer for meeting with you

- ☐ Shake the interviewer's hand before departing

- ☐ Send a thank you for the interview email
  - ■ State that you are interested in the position
  - ■ State that you would welcome the opportunity to become a part of their organization

Workplace Readiness

- ☐ When you accept a job offer you make a commitment to your employer

- ☐ Arriving for work on time
    - ■ Arriving for work on time requires planning
    - ■ Adjust your sleeping habits
        - ☐ Have a set time to go to bed every night

        - ☐ Turn off your cell phone before you go to bed

            - ☐ It is easy to loose track of time when texting and talking on the phone
        - ☐ Turn off the television, radio and light

            - ☐ Your sense of hearing is still being used while you are sleeping
            - ☐ Deep sleep comes from sleeping in darkness

- ☐ Plan your morning routine before you go to bed each night
  - ■ Prepare your clothes for the next day
  - ■ Select and iron your clothes every night
  - ■ Charge your cell phone
  - ■ Pack your lunch

- ☐ Create a morning schedule
  - ■ Get up when the alarm clock goes off
  - ■ Do not press the snooze button
    - ☐ A five minute snooze can easily turn into 15 minutes or a half hour
  - ■ Schedule a time to review your text and voicemail messages each morning

Plan Your Travel

- ☐ Your employer expects you to arrive for work on time
  - ■ If you plan your travel
    - ☐ It will ensure you arrive on time
    - ☐ It will help to reduce your stress
  - ■ Have an alternate travel route

- ☐ There are always transportation delays
- ☐ You should know two ways of travel to and from your destination
- ■ Schedule extra time into your travel schedule
  - ☐ This will allow for the unexpected delays that could potentially make you arrive late

Technology Usage

- ☐ Telephone usage
  - ■ You should not use the telephone at your place of work for personal calls
  - ■ It is also inappropriate to use your cell phone during work hours
    - ☐ You should wait until your lunch hour to send and respond to text and email messages sent to your cell phone

- ☐ Computer usage
  - ■ Do not use your workplace computer for personal entertainment

- Do no check your personal email account
- Do not check your social media accounts

☐ The computer assigned to you is for work purposes only

Things to remember

☐ Lunch time
  - Do not exceed the amount of time that you are given for lunch
  - Return from lunch at your scheduled time

☐ Dress code
  - Follow the dress code policy of the company
  - Ask questions if you are unsure

☐ Time off from work
  - If you need time off from work, notify your supervisor in advance (when possible)
  - If you have an unexpected absence, telephone your workplace and speak with your supervisor before your start time
  - Be responsible when taking time off

☐ Too many unexpected absences will make you appear to be unreliable

Time Management

Time management is essential when aspiring to achieve goals and productivity

Time management is....
- ☐ The act of demonstrating that you have control over the amount of time spent on a specific task or goal.
- ☐ Are you effectively managing your time?
  - ■ Are you getting everything accomplished on time?

- ☐ Time management facts

- ☐ All of us are given the same amount of time each day (24 hours)
  - ■ Typically full-time employees work between 7 and 8 hours daily
  - ■ Typically part-time employees work between 4 and 6 hours daily
  - ■ High School students work hours in accordance to Labor Laws for their age

- ☐ We all use our time differently

- ☐ People put their time and energy into activities that are of value or important to them such as:

- Having full-time or part-time employment
- Having opportunities for workplace advancement

☐ Time management requires you to evaluate yourself, change old habits and create new habits through a self assessment (this is known as personal growth)
☐ Poor time management
- Will make you appear to be unreliable and/or irresponsible
- Is sometimes associated with immaturity
- Will make you appear to lack interest
- Will contribute to being overlooked for new opportunities

☐ What prevents you from using your time wisely?
- Procrastinating
  - Delaying work on an assignment until the last minute
- Socializing with co-workers
- Using work technology for personal business
- Talking on your cell phone during work hours

- Underestimating the amount of time needed to complete a task
  - Rushing to complete work assignments based upon an unrealistic self imposed timeframe
- Lack of organization
  - Not thinking/planning how to complete a project
  - Failing to review instructions for an assignment
  - Not allowing time to ask questions and follow-up when instructions seem unclear

- Reactive vs. proactive behavior
  - Lacking the ability to manage your emotions due to the stress associated with delaying work on an assignment
  - Thinking negatively instead of positively to resolve a situation
    - There is nothing I can do (negative) vs. let me look at my options (positive)
    - I can't do this assignment (negative) vs. I can find a way to do this assignment (positive)

- Concealing the problem from your supervisor (negative) vs. admitting you are not meeting expectations for completing a project and seeking help from your supervisor (positive)

Effective Time Management Techniques

☐ Make a list
  - write down the things that you need to accomplish on a daily basis
  - Schedule a time to work on each task

☐ Check off completed tasks
  - once you complete a task, place a check mark next to the task on your list

☐ Status notes
  - write notes on your list that relate to the unaccomplished tasks
  - status notes should include what has been completed and what remains to be done
  - this will help you to remember where to begin the next time you work on this task

- ☐ Limit distractions
    - ■ distractions are the number one reason why goals are not fulfilled and assignment completion is delayed
    - ■ while it is impossible to plan for the unexpected, it is not impossible to make a plan to reduce distractions

- ☐ Focus on your work assignments
    - ■ Do not take breaks that include socializing with your co-workers
    - ■ Do not text, make personal calls and use the computer for personal activities

- ☐ If you attending school while working, schedule time to study
    - ■ make a schedule with specific dates and times to study

- ☐ Create a place to study
    - ■ set up an area to serve as your study location
    - ■ make sure that you have all of your supplies (school books, paper and pens) in your study area

- ☐ Make a study plan

- write down the subjects you plan to work on during the time you are scheduled to study
- this will help you to stay on task
- your plan should include specific goals
  - for example you may decide to complete the math homework that is due next week
  - or perhaps you may decide to read the history chapter that you began in school today

☐ Turn off your cell phone, television and radio
- the best way to focus on a task is to eliminate all distractions
- turning off these items will allow you to focus

☐ Schedule a break
- if you are planning to study for a couple of hours, it is important that you schedule short breaks so that your mind does not wonder
- schedule a 15 minute snack break or a few minutes to stretch your arms and legs

- breaks should never include watching television, texting or speaking to your friends on the telephone

☐ Be selective about the friends you study with
  - **only study with friends who are serious about studying**
  - if you decide to study with a friend, please make sure that you discuss what you will be studying in advance
  - do not study with friends who use doing homework and/or studying as an opportunity to socialize with you

☐ Time Management Recap

☐ Evaluate yourself, change old habits and create new habits

☐ Be **proactive** not reactive

☐ Set get goals/make a list of things to be accomplished with a specific timeframe attached to each goal

☐ If you encounter a problem ask for help

☐ Remember to always do your best!

Social Media – Things You Should Know

☐ Almost everyone uses a form of social media
- Social media such as LinkedIn is typically used for employment advanced

☐ There are other forms of social media that are typically used for sharing social information
- Facebook
- Instagram
- Twitter
- Tumblr
- Blogs

☐ This list is certain to grow and some of these social media reference may be outdated when this book is published

☐ Below are some important facts about social media

☐ Social media is a growing industry
- This industry thrives on the participation of young adults
- Legal ownership of information and pictures posted to social media sites has not been clearly defined

- ☐ Some employers conduct social media background checks on candidates that they are interested in hiring

- ☐ Social media background checks are typically referred to as social intelligence conduct or background investigations

- ☐ Some employers may ask you to sign a release that allows the company to conduct a social intelligence conduct or background investigation
    - ■ Signing a release could potentially eliminate a company's liability if/when
    - ■ A social intelligence conduct or background investigation provides what a company may believe to be questionable behavior
    - ■ The engagement in activities that could potential adversely impact the company's reputation
    - ■ A decision is made not hire a candidate based upon this information
    - ■ There are several companies that perform social intelligence conduct and background investigations. Below is a short list of the companies:
        - ▪ Social Intelligence

- InfoCheckUSA
- Tandem Select

Volunteer Work

Volunteer work offers a great opportunity to obtain work experience and build your resume. Below are organizations with volunteer opportunities:

The Red Cross
www.myredcross.org
email: youthvolunteers@myredcross.org
ages 14 – 18

American Museum of Natural History
www.amnh.org
ages: 16+

American Society for the Prevention of Cruelty to Animals (ASPCA)
www.aspca.org
ages: 16+

Children's Museum of Manhattan
High School Internship Program
www.cmom.org
look under outreach opportunities and internship
ages: high school sophomores, juniors and seniors
Earth Celebrations

Community Environment Arts Projects
www.earthcelebrations.com
email@earthcelebrations.com

ages: all ages

Food Bank for New York City
www.foodbanknyc.org
volunteer@foodbanknyc.org
ages: 16+

Idealist
Website that post various volunteer opportunities
www.idealist.org
ages: all ages

Lighthouse International
*Read weekly or act as a substitute reader for the
visually impaired*
www.lighthouse.org
rsaunders@lighthouse.org
ages: 16+

Project Reach Youth
Teen Leadership and Peer Education Programs
www.pry.org
ages: 13+

Village Temple Soup Kitchen
Saturday morning meal preparation
www.villagetemple.org
646-857-8258 (soup kitchen)
ages: various

Visiting Neighbors
Visiting with seniors and serving a shopping and errand escorts
www.visitingneighbors.org
ages: 15 – 18+

Monitoring Your Credit

☐ Protect yourself from identity thief

- The three credit bureaus (Experian, Equifax and Trans Union) have jointly set-up a website so that the public can order their free credit reports over the internet.

- The website is www.annualcreditreport.com You may also request your free reports by calling: 1-877-322-8228 or you can contact each of the credit bureaus separately:

Experian
Telephone: 888-397-3742
Website: www.experian.com

Equifax
Telephone: 800-685-1111
Website: www.equifax.com

Trans Union
Telephone: 800-888-4213
Website: www.transunion.com

- ☐ When ordering your credit report, you will be asked to provide the following information:
  - ■ First, middle and last name
  - ■ Current address and previous addresses for the past five years
  - ■ Social Security number
  - ■ Date of birth

- ☐ Once you receive your credit report confirm it is completely accurate by:
  - ■ Confirming the accuracy of the spelling of your name
  - ■ Confirm that current and previous addresses are places that you actually lived
  - ■ Confirm the information in the employment section is accurate
  - ■ Confirm that the accounts listed on your report are actually accounts that you opened

- ☐ Confirm the information about your accounts is accurate by reviewing the following for each account:

  - ■ Balance
  - ■ Date opened
  - ■ Payment Status
  - ■ Account Type
  - ■ Credit Limit

- Terms
- Past Due
- Payment history (pay close attention to late payments and payment history)
- Contact the credit bureaus if you note incorrect entries on your credit reports
- Follow-up with the credit bureaus to confirm that the changes have been made

Managing Your Finances

- ☐ Once you begin earning an income monitor your finances
- ☐ Create a monthly budget
- ☐ Know your monthly income
- ☐ Monitor how much money you spend
- ☐ Keep receipts for your purchases
- ☐ Keep ATM withdrawal receipts
- ☐ Document your financial transaction in writing
- ☐ Write down deposits and withdrawals from your bank accounts
- ☐ Review your credit card statements monthly
- ☐ Do not spend all of your money
- ☐ Set monthly savings goals
- ☐ Learn the difference between things that are necessities and luxuries

- ☐ Remember to be **S.M.A.R.T**. when managing your finances

S = spend wisely

M = make monthly budget

A = act financially responsible

R = remember your spending today affects your credit in the future

T = talk to a responsible adult if you get into financial trouble

Void Becoming a Credit Repair Scam Victim

- ☐ There are numerous companies and organizations that claim to help people repair their credit

    - ■ Some of these companies and organizations are not reputable

    - ■ The National Foundation For Credit Counseling (NFCC) is a non-profit counseling can refer to you a member organization that will be able to provide you with guidance on how to begin to repair your credit

        - ▪ Website: http://www.nfcc.org/

- ☐ Research your rights:
    - ▪ Avoid companies that do not advise you of your legal rights

- ☐ Below is a short list of signs that a credit counseling company is trying to scam you:

    - ▪ Avoid companies that want you to pay for credit repair services before they have provided any service

- Payment should not be rendered until the services have been provided

- Avoid companies that do not inform you of the things you can do to repair your credit yourself free

- Avoid companies that advise you dispute accurate information on our credit report and to take actions that seem illegal

☐ There is no legal way to "repair" credit
  - You cannot erase your credit history

☐ You can improve your credit by doing the following:

  - **Make payment arrangements with creditors**

  - Establish a payment plan that you can adhere to

☐ Making corrections to inaccurate entries your credit report

- ☐ Develop / maintain a history of making monthly payments on time (or according to payment arrangements made with a creditor)

Meet The Author

Dawn Brangman

- ☐ Founder of MyBrandMyStyle, LLC
  A professional development organization
  for young adults in high school and
  college
  - ■ Website: mybrandmystyle.com
  - ■ Email:
    aboutus@mybrandmystyle.com

- ☐ Education:
  - ■ Bachelor of Science
    Business, Management & Economics
  - ■ Master of Arts
    Labor and Policy Studies

- ☐ Experience
  - ■ 20+ years of experiences working
    with young adults in high school
    and college
  - ■ Develops and manages intern
    programs for high school and
    college students
  - ■ Collaborates with public and
    private schools to host professional
    development seminars for high
    school and college students